W9-AKD-937

A New True Book

THE INDIAN OCEAN

By Susan Heinrichs

CHILDRENS PRESS ®

CHICAGO

Beach on the Indian Ocean

Dedicated to Michael

Library of Congress Cataloging-in-Publication Data

Heinrichs, Susan.
    The Indian Ocean.

    (A New true book)
    Includes index.
    Summary: Describes features of the Indian Ocean,
including its plants, animals, and volcanic activity.
    1. Indian Ocean—Juvenile literature. [1.   Indian
Ocean. 2. Ocean] I. Title.
GC721.H43 1986   910'.09165   86-9579
ISBN 0-516-01293-2

PHOTO CREDITS

© Cameramann International, Ltd.—8
(2 photos), 44 (bottom left)

Historical Pictures Service—4
(2 photos), 16

Journalism Services: © David
Waselle—27 (top left, bottom left,
bottom right), 29 (2 photos)

Odyssey Productions
© Bob Frerck—Cover, 11, 42, 43 (left),
44 (right)
© Charles Seaborn—32 (top left)

Photri—2, 9 (left), 21, 32 (center
right), 38

Root Resources: © John Hoellen—44
(top left)

© James P. Rowan—22

Tom Stack & Associates:
© J. Cancalosi—32 (top right)
© Gerald A. Corsi—37 (right)
© M. P. Kahl—37 (left), 40
© Brian Parker—28 (top), 30 (bottom
left), 32 (center left and bottom right),
33
© Ed. Robinson—28 (bottom)
© Carl Roessler—26, 30 (bottom right)
© Tom Stack—25, 27 (top right), 35
© William Stephens—30 (top)
© Jack D. Swenson—39
© John Webber—43 (right), 45

© Lynn Stone—41

Valan Photos, Inc.: © F. Yuwono—44
(top right)

Maps: Albert R. Mangus—7, 9 (right),
13, 19

Cover: Coastal dhows, Lamu, Kenya

TABLE OF CONTENTS

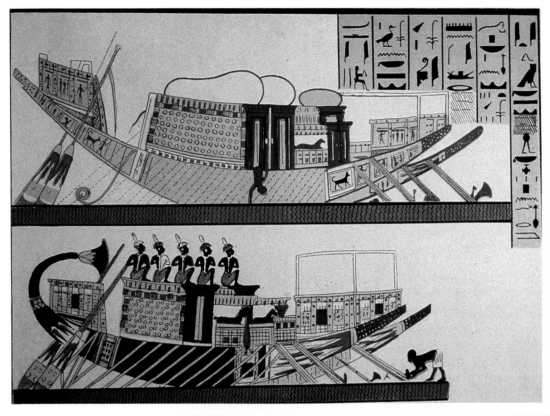

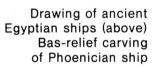

Drawing of ancient
Egyptian ships (above)
Bas-relief carving
of Phoenician ship

4

THE SMALLEST OCEAN

More than a thousand years before the birth of Christ, Egyptian, Phoenician, and Indian sailors traveled up and down the Indian Ocean. Later, Chinese and Arabic sailors came. All came to fish and trade goods with the countries around the Indian Ocean.

Hundreds of years later explorers from Europe

came to the Indian Ocean. The most famous explorer was Vasco da Gama. In 1497 he left his home in Portugal and sailed south. Da Gama rounded the tip of Africa, crossed the Indian Ocean, and landed in India. This was the first time anyone from Europe had traveled to India by sea.

The Indian Ocean is small. It is bordered on all

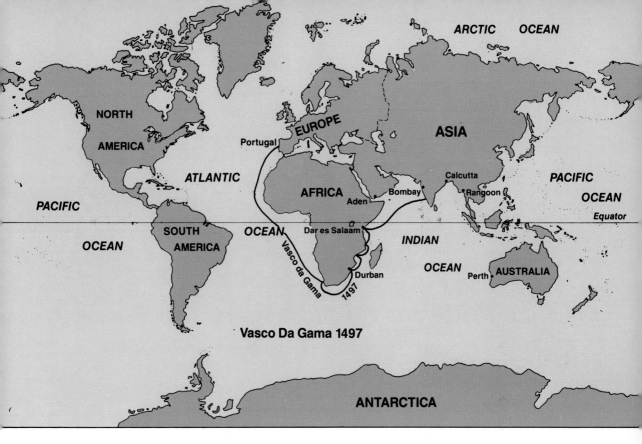

Vasco Da Gama 1497

sides by continents—Asia,
Australia, Antarctica, and
Africa. Many important
seaports and cities are
built on the shores of the
Indian Ocean.

7

Arab dhows (above) and cargo ships (left)

The Indian Ocean is a
busy place. Arab ships
called dhows still sail its
waters. Newer ships carry
oil and other goods from
port to port. Many ships
cross the Indian Ocean to

The Suez Canal (left) connects the Indian Ocean
and the Red Sea with the Mediterranean Sea.

get to the Suez Canal. This
famous canal gives ships
a short water passage to
the Mediterranean Sea and
Europe. Before the Suez
Canal was built in 1869,
ships had to make the
long trip around Africa.

TIDES AND CURRENTS

Big slow movements of a whole ocean are called tides. The sun and moon pull on the water in the oceans. They pull the water up toward the land. Then they pull it back. Water pulled toward the land is called flood tide. Water pulled away from the land is called an ebb tide.

Fishing boats in Sri Lanka

As on all oceans, tides rise and fall twice a day on the Indian Ocean. But because the ocean is small, its tides do not change as much as they do on the Atlantic or Pacific oceans.

In some places, people wait for the Indian Ocean's tide to go out. Then they walk along the shore looking for food left by the ebb tide.

Sometimes only parts of the ocean move. Movements from big parts of the ocean are called currents. Currents are caused partly by the wind swirling the water. In the

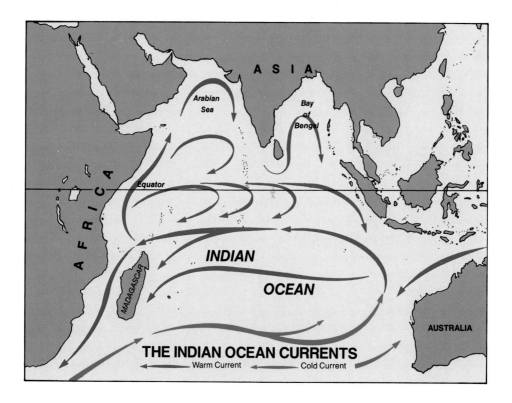

THE INDIAN OCEAN CURRENTS
Warm Current ← → Cold Current

Indian Ocean, the wind and waters swirl in one direction for six months. Then the wind changes. It swirls the water in the other direction for the next six months.

13

EARTHQUAKES AND VOLCANOES

The waves in the Indian Ocean are caused mostly by the wind. But sometimes they are caused by other things.

Once in a while, a chunk of sand or rock on the bottom of the Indian Ocean caves in. This causes an earthquake. Sometimes an underwater mountain rumbles and

This volcanic island was born in 1925. It is still growing from volcanic activity.

shakes. Then it spews out melted rocks and gas. This is called a volcano.

Volcanoes and earthquakes jolt the Indian Ocean so much that a huge wave begins. An enormous wave caused by

Krakatoa

underwater earthquakes
and volcanoes is called a
tsunami.

There is a volcano
named Krakatoa in the
northeast part of the Indian
Ocean. One day in 1883,

it began shooting out
rocks, gas, and ashes. it
continued all day and
night. The next morning it
erupted with one great
blast. It made probably the
loudest noise since the
earth began. People heard
it three thousand miles
away.

After the blast, some
people went outside to see
all the dust and ash. They
did not know that the

volcano had jolted the
ocean. They did not know
that huge waves were
coming toward them. When
the tsunamis hit land, they
killed 36,000 people. Some
waves were so strong that
they crossed the Indian
Ocean, went around Africa,
and continued across the
Atlantic Ocean.

SECRETS OF THE FLOOR

The bottom of the ocean
is called the floor. There
are chains of mountains
along the floor. There are
deep cracks called
trenches. There are also

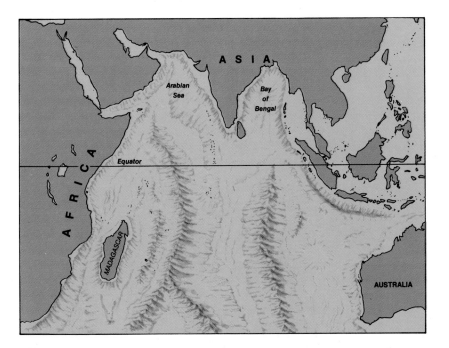

wide flat spaces called abyssal plains.

Scientists have found all sorts of things on the floor of the Indian Ocean. They see ash left from volcanoes. They discover parts of dead ocean animals. Divers find diamonds on the floor near Africa. In some places, there are even particles from outer space. These pieces landed in the Indian Ocean and slowly drifted to the bottom. This debris

Diver filming with an underwater camera

is thousands of feet thick
in some areas.

Pretend you could dig
into the ocean floor. First,
you would find sand and
dead animals and plants
that landed just this year.
As you dug deeper and
deeper, you would find
older and older objects.

Fossil fish

Traces of dead plants
and animals are called
fossils. Dead plants and
animals have landed on
the Indian Ocean's floor for
a long, long time.
Sometimes scientists find
fossils from plants and
animals that lived millions
of years ago.

STRANGE LIGHTS AND COLORS

Most of the Indian Ocean's plants are tiny. They have no roots or leaves. They float near the surface and grow in the sunlight. The surface waters are loaded with these plants. Many fish and other animals eat them. Fish swim through the water with their mouths open and get an easy meal.

There is one tiny creature that is very common in the Indian Ocean. It is called a dinoflagellate. Many types of dinoflagellates need sunlight to grow, like plants. But dinoflagellates can also swim like animals. Nobody is quite sure what they are.

Some dinoflagellates are very colorful. Sometimes there are so many red ones in the Indian Ocean that the water looks red.

Dinoflagellate

People call this water red
tide.

Other dinoflagellates
glow in the dark. People
thought the dinoflagellates
ground together salt grains
from the water to make
sparks. But that is not true.
They glow because of
special chemicals in their
bodies.

Diver explores a fish-filled reef.

ANIMAL LIFE

The Indian Ocean is a warm ocean and its waters are rich with ocean life. Its coral islands shelter

sponges, worms, crabs, sea
urchins, starfish, and
millions of tiny, colorful
coral fish.

Christmas tree worms on coral (left),
clownfish (bottom left),
starfish (bottom right),
long-nose hawkfish (below)

Coral polyp

Sponge crab

The porcupine fish (left)
defends itself by inflating
its spines (above).

Some unusual fish make
their home in the Indian
Ocean. The porcupine fish
is covered with spines.
When an enemy threatens,
the fish inflates with air,
and its spines stand
straight out.

Flying fish (above) and cuttlefish (below)
are common in the Indian Ocean.

Flying fish are also found. These fish have large fins near their heads. They use them to leap out of the water and soar through the air.

Cuttlefish are very common too. They really are not fish at all. Cuttlefish are related to the octopuses. They squirt ink from their body in

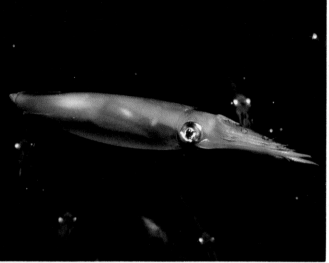

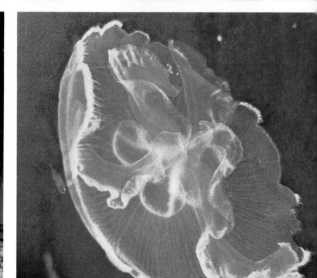

Squid (top left), Australian sea lions (top right), white-tip shark (middle left), jellyfish (middle right), and green sea turtle (right) swim in the Indian Ocean.

Bottlenose
dolphin

order to confuse enemies
and to hide their escape.

Jellyfish, squid,
anchovies, sailfish, sea
turtles, and several kinds
of sharks also swim in the
Indian Ocean.

Large sea mammals,
such as dolphins and seals
can also be found.

A LIVING FOSSIL

In 1938, fishermen in the
Indian Ocean caught a
very strange fish. It was
big and bulky. Its fins
were thick, fleshy paddles.
Scientists had found fossil
skeletons of this fish
earlier. They thought it
died out millions of years
ago. But here was a living
fish called a coelacanth.
Only a few more

Close-up of
a coelacanth

coelacanths have been
caught since then.

Animals from the
deepest part of the ocean
live in the dark and cold.

They have tons and tons of seawater pressing down on them. Their bodies must be strong to live under all that pressure. People sometimes bring them up from the very deep. Then there is no more pressure. Their bodies just fall apart.

Royal albatross (left) and
frigate bird (right)

FISHING EXPERTS

Many birds, such as the albatross and frigate bird, get their food from the Indian Ocean. Some birds have long bills. They walk out into the water and catch little fish.

Pelican

Other birds fish together in groups. Pelicans swim out and form half circles in the water. Then they swim toward the shore. Fish get trapped in the half circle and are quickly eaten.

Shearwater in its nest

Shearwaters are birds
that fly along the coasts of
Madagascar and eastern
Africa. People see them
catch flying fish as they
soar into the air.

Flamingos live around
Africa's tip. They feed by
putting their heads upside

Flamingos

down in pools of water.
Then they swing their
heads back and forth to
filter out small plants and
animals.

Herons are birds with
long skinny legs. They
wade out from the shore
to catch fish.

Egrets are members of the heron family. They are found in the Indian Ocean.

Fishermen of Sri Lanka have learned a thing or two from the herons. The fishermen wade out from the shore, too. They jab the ends of long wooden poles into the sandy floor.

Fishing on stilts in Sri Lanka

They climb the poles and stand on little platforms. Then they cast their fishing lines into the water. Water washes around their stilts. The fishermen don't wobble either.

Marine Drive (left) in Bombay, India and
fishing nets (right) in Cochin, India

The Indian Ocean has
been an important part of
people's lives for
thousands of years.
Explorers sailed across it
long before anyone thought
of crossing any other

Skyline of Perth on the west coast of Australia (above left),
fishermen in west Java (above right), colorful umbrella on the
beach near Trivandrum, India (below left), and Indian Ocean
near Port Elizabeth, Australia (below right)

oceans. This seaway
became an easy way to
get from one city to
another. Many people still
depend on the Indian
Ocean for their food.

In some ways the Indian
Ocean will always be a
strange and mysterious
place. There is so much
more to learn about it.

WORDS YOU SHOULD KNOW

coelacanth(SEEL • uh • kanth) — a very ancient type of fish, once thought to be extinct

currents(KUR • unts) — ocean movements caused by winds, the heat of the sun, or the earth's movements

dinoflagellate(dine • oh • FLAJ • uh • late) — a tiny sea organism that is partly like an animal and partly like a plant

earthquake(ERTH • kwayk) — a trembling of the ground caused by movements within the earth

Krakatoa(krack • uh • TOE • uh) — an island in Indonesia which was destroyed in 1884 by a volcano on the island

oceanographer(oh • shun • AH • gruh • fur) — a scientist who studies oceans and ocean life

Suez Canal(SOO • ez kuh • NAL) — a manmade waterway between the Mediterranean Sea and the Red Sea

tides(TYDZ) — ocean movements caused by the pull of the moon and sun, causing flood tide (a flooding of the shore) and ebb tide (water pulled away from the shore)

tsunami(soo • NAH • mee) — a massive wave caused by a volcano or an earthquake on the ocean floor

volcano(vol • KAY • no) — a crack in the earth's crust through which melted rock and steam pour out

waves(WAYVZ) — ocean movements caused by wind or underwater earthquakes or volcanos

INDEX

About the author

  Susan Heinrichs holds a Master of Science degree in zoology
with a specialty in aquatic biology, and studied marine biology at
Duke University Marine Research Lab. Her articles have appeared
in several scientific journals. As a consultant to the U.S. Army
Corps of Engineers, she formulated environmental impact
statements and researched zooplankton species in man-made
lakes. Her research activities at the National Reservoir Research
Center have included investigating trout kills on Arkansas rivers
and coordinating research and data on reservoirs nationwide.
  Ms. Heinrichs has taught general and aquatic biology, human
anatomy and physiology, and animation at the Universities of
Arkansas and Oklahoma. A photographer, electron microscopist,
and scientific illustrator, she has published illustrations in
numerous journals. She currently owns her own graphic arts
business in Norman, Oklahoma, and is directing and shooting
instructional video tapes for electron microscopy students.